The EYFS Inspection in practice

Your step by step guide to the new Common Inspection Framework

By Jenny Barber and Sharon Paul-Smith

Introduction — 2
The Common Inspection Framework (CIF) — 2
and the key judgements

Reflective practice — 4

The Self-Evaluation Form (SEF) — 7

Preparing for inspection — 10
Paperwork and systems checklist — 11
Prevent Duty guidance — 14
British Values — 15
Quality improvement plan — 19

'First impressions count' — 29

Step by step guide to completing your SEF — 34

The inspection day — 46
Compliance checklist for inspection — 46

Practitioners and the inspection — 52

After the inspection — 54

Further resources — 57

Photocopiable forms
British Values in your setting — 17
Quality of teaching evidence checklist — 18-19
The effectiveness of leadership and — 20-21
management of the early years provision
Teaching, learning and assessment — 22-23
Personal development, behaviour and welfare — 24-25
Outcomes for children — 26
Training records — 27-28
'First impressions' checklist — 32-33

Published by Practical Pre-School Books, A Division of MA Education Ltd, St Jude's Church, Dulwich Road, Herne Hill, London, SE24 0PB
Tel: 0207 738 5454
www.practicalpreschoolbooks.com
© 2015 MA Education Ltd.
Front cover photo by Lucie Carlier, © MA Education Ltd.
Illustrated by Cathy Hughes.

The EYFS Inspection in practice ISBN 978-1-909280-87-8

Introduction

The Common Inspection Framework (CIF) aligns inspections across all of the different education remits, with four common inspection judgements. The purpose of the CIF is to provide consistency and comparability across all the types of provision that Ofsted inspects. Each type of provision has its own remit specific inspection handbook. It is the Early Years Inspection Handbook to which we refer in this book.

The four judgements for inspection are:

- Effectiveness of leadership and management

- Quality of teaching, learning and assessment

- Personal development, behaviour and welfare

- Outcomes for children and learners.

Inspectors will also make a judgment on the effectiveness of safeguarding.

In the new inspection framework there is greater emphasis on the importance of leadership and the decisions you make and the impact on the children.

The book is set out in clear chapters to guide you through the processes of the inspection, with checklists and reference charts for you and your staff to work through.

Reflective practice

We begin with reflective practice, as this is an essential tool for continual development within a setting, both for individuals and the setting as a whole. The skills and awareness that are honed through reflective practice will support both the completion of the SEF and, going forward, look at how to develop practice following your inspection.

The SEF

The chapter on the SEF has comprehensive grids, guiding you through each section of the SEF with suggestions and points for consideration to help you complete the SEF relevantly and constructively. These grids provide a detailed explanation of the questions posed in the Ofsted Early Years Self Evaluation Guidance document. Additionally, there are suggestions for evidence that you could make available to back up your statements.

OVERVIEW OF THE FOUR JUDGEMENTS

EFFECTIVENESS OF LEADERSHIP AND MANAGEMENT
- Emphasis on the curriculum
- Teaching and learning in the curriculum
- Ambitious vision, ethos and culture
- Safeguarding
- Supervision
- School readiness
- British values
- Behaviour

QUALITY OF TEACHING, LEARNING AND ASSESSMENT
- Evidence of different kinds of assessment
- Parent involvement
- Teaching and learning

PERSONAL DEVELOPMENT, BEHAVIOUR AND WELFARE
- Consistent safeguarding
- Keeps safe
- Self awareness
- Going beyond welfare requirements
- Behaviour/interactions
- Evidence children understand personal development, behaviour and welfare
- Independence
- Next stages of learning

OUTCOMES FOR CHILDREN AND LEARNERS
- Progress from starting points for individuals and groups
- Helping children catch up
- Best fit for all
- Quality of teaching and impact on progress and achievement

How to prepare for the day

We then move onto other preparations you may need to make for an inspection: your general principles of good practice for all visitors to your setting and the involvement of all practitioners working in the setting. These are explored in the chapters 'First impressions count' and 'Preparing for your inspection.' A first impressions checklist will help you to objectively look at supporting your own setting and identify how a visitor might see it. We have included a compliance checklist and a systems checklist to help ensure you have in place all the necessary processes and paperwork.

The inspection day

The chapter 'The inspection day' explores how to cope on the day and support staff as well as the importance of paying close attention to the feedback you receive from the inspector. 'After the inspection' looks at how you can take your practice forward and move on, regardless of your grading outcome.

This book is designed to enable anyone working in the early years to ensure their EYFS inspection is a positive and stress-free experience.

Reflective practice

In the DfES publication 'Key Elements for Effective Practice' (2005), it states that:

'Effective practice in the early years requires committed, enthusiastic and reflective practitioners with a breadth and depth of knowledge, skills and understanding.'

Additionally in the Ofsted publication 'Childcare groups: a passion to be outstanding' (2009) it states that:

'Outstanding providers told us that reflective practice is crucial to their success. They are not complacent but aspire continually to do better. They regularly review what they do and how this helps children.'

For a long time it has been considered good practice for practitioners to 'reflect on their own practice'. It is a phrase widely used, but what does it mean exactly and how should we reflect? There are in fact two terms that you should be familiar with: reflective practice and reflective practitioners.

Reflective practice

This means thinking about and analysing your actions and practice with a view to changing, developing and improving practice.

Reflective practitioner

This describes a practitioner who is aware of their strengths and skills, as well as their knowledge gaps and areas for skill development – and are ready to work on them.

So, it is not just being aware of what you do and what your strengths and skills are, it is about taking action and moving forward. It is about identifying what you could do differently, how you could better support the children and work more effectively with your team.

There are many benefits to reflective practice and being a reflective practitioner.

Benefits for the individual include:

■ Skills are developed.

■ More motivated.

■ Greater job satisfaction.

■ Personal development.

■ Become an agent of change.

■ Better able to meet the needs of children and their families.

■ More confident.

■ Able to meet challenges presented within the job role.

■ Stronger professional relationships within the team.

Benefits for the children:

■ Their individual needs are more likely to be effectively met.

■ The learning environment will better meet their needs.

■ Practitioners have a greater understanding of how to support development and fill in any gaps.

Benefits for the setting:

■ A more effective setting with highly skilled and motivated staff.

■ Staff feel more valued.

■ Children are happy and settled as their needs are met and supported, leading to happy parents and a good reputation for the setting.

- More organised and efficient.

- Staff become agents of change and ensure that the setting is constantly evolving and developing.

- The setting is perceived to be innovative with a focused vision.

So the benefits may well be numerous, but how do you start to be a reflective practitioner? For purposeful and effective reflective practice, we need to invest time in the process, so that it becomes part of everyone's way of working.

Most people are already doing it without realising it. The observations we carry out, the reflection on children's needs and interests and how we use that information to inform planning are all partial reflections, and the skills honed through that practice can help us to be good reflective practitioners.

We need to begin assessing ourselves, the need to do what we do and how we do it; remembering to be completely truthful. Reflective practice is never going to be truly effective unless we are 100% honest with ourselves about what we do, remembering there is a distinct difference between what we might say or think we do and what we actually do. Reflection is like putting a mirror up to your work and seeing from the reverse viewpoint what you are doing.

Some practitioners may need additional support to look clearly into the mirror, and identify what it is they say they do and what they actually do. This necessary support will largely depend on their learning style and ability to objectively analyse.

Let's begin with some straightforward basic questions about ourselves as positive role models and then move on to our knowledge, awareness and understanding of individual key children.

Reflect on your practice in relation to these questions about being a positive

role model; remember to ask yourself – be honest and truthful.

- I always say hello and good morning to the people around me.
- I offer to help other staff members set up or tidy away.

- I always say please and thank you.

- I am patient.

- I like to help people.

- I listen to other people's points of view.

- I am tidy and organised.

Having done that, you can then move on to thinking about a specific child. Your perception might be, as with the questions above, that you do that all the time, but do you? Choose one of your key children as an example:

How often do you smile and acknowledge the child positively?

How much time do you spend listening to and talking to the child?

What type of activities does the child enjoy most?

How do you use these activities to help the child learn?

Having eased yourself in, you can then begin to delve into specific aspects of your work using the following techniques to help you gain an insight.

- To begin with, you need to question what you do, why you do it and how you do it. Then think about your thoughts and responses. This might be done individually or as a team.

- Could it be done differently: are there alternatives that could be better or more effective? Ask 'what if?'. Test new ideas, maybe visit other settings to gain a different insight and perspective.

- Remember to be open-minded: don't just assume a new way of doing something won't necessarily work, have a go and see what happens, you might be surprised.

- As you seek alternatives consider the different points of views of those involved/affected e.g. parents, children, other staff.

- Use reflective practice to identify and resolve issues, using a problem solving approach.

There are many aspects of practice that can be considered e.g. partnership with parents, snack time, management of behaviour, hygiene routines, child initiated opportunities in the outside environment.

EYFS Themes

EYFS Theme: A Unique Child

What activities or experiences in the setting help children to think about:

- The things that make them feel good about themselves?

- The people who help them?

- How to keep themselves safe?

- How to recognise and avoid possible danger?

- Reasons for making particular choices?

- The reason they are allowed to do or to have some things and not other things?

EYFS Theme: Enabling Environments

- How well do you reflect examples of outdoor learning in your observations and assessments of children?

- Does indoor provision meet the needs of all the children as both a place to feel at home and a place to learn?

- How do you ensure that the deployment of staff is flexible enough to respond to the flow and movement of children between indoors and outdoors?

EYFS Theme: Creating and thinking critically

- What open-ended activities do you provide for children in your setting?

- Do you give children the experience of playing with paint and glue before expecting them to use them to make a Christmas card?

- Have you ever recorded your interactions with children to see how you support the development of creativity and critical thinking?

Supporting your team

- How do you ensure that team members understand their roles and responsibilities?

- How do you support members of the team in their work?

- Do you actively recognise an individual's strengths?

- How often do you provide feedback on staff performance?

- How do you ensure that their work is interesting and valuable?

- Do you encourage team members to take on responsibility?

- How do you ensure that team members are able to extend their knowledge, skills and experience?

- Do you act upon things that have been said to you, are you seen as being pro-active?

- What opportunities have you provided for staff to contribute new ideas and develop their capabilities?

It isn't sufficient to simply ask the questions and reflect on your practice: you then have to take action to develop practice and move forward. You need to identify how this can be done, who will need to be involved and whether any additional support or training will be required.

Keeping records of discussions on reflective practice and documenting how you are going to move forward, shows good practice in relation to self-assessment.

This can be done in two ways, as the individual or the team/setting as a whole. Records kept as part of the appraisal and supervision process will show how the individual is a reflective practitioner. For the team or setting as a whole, the easiest way to do this is to complete an action plan, identifying what you need to develop in terms of practice. The targets set in the action plan must be **SMART**:

Specific – clearly identified as actions.

Measurable – it must clearly show it can be seen that the actions have been achieved or not.

Achievable – practitioners can work easily to achieve them.

Realistic – all the necessary tools need to be available so the actions can be achieved.

Time bound – a date identified when the actions need to be achieved by or identifying when there will be a review.

Failing to act upon what has been identified through reflective practice

can have a demotivating effect, so the follow through action is essential. This is particularly important for managers supporting practitioners in the setting.

As practitioners become more aware and reflective practice skills are developed, they may wish to keep a reflective practice diary. This type of diary can be a record of what is useful to you and a memory cue. It may describe significant incidents relating to practice and facilitate evaluation of these incidents and implications for practice.

Becoming a reflective practitioner as previously stated gives a much clearer insight into an individual's role, and once this insight has evolved, more searching questions can be asked.

- How do I see my role?

- What kind of practitioner do I think I am: what are my key skills and strengths?

- What are my personal thoughts on the role of early years education?

- How do I show that I am consistent at all times in my practice?

Once reflective practice becomes integral to what happens within the setting, the benefits will quickly become clear, and practitioners will as a result be committed to achieving high standards in all aspects of practice.

Inspectors will focus on how well leaders and managers use performance management and self evaluation to provide a focus for professional development.

The Self-Evaluation Form (SEF)

The inspector will talk to you about your SEF, to test the accuracy of this as a self reflection tool and your knowledge of quality improvement needs.

Why is there now so much emphasis on the Self-Evaluation Form (SEF)? Research has proven that self-reflection and evaluation both support good practice within a setting as part of continual development. Importantly, this self-reflection supports good outcomes for children.

The EPPE (Effective Provision of Pre-School Education) project was very influential in informing us of the significance of self-reflection and evaluation.

'The use of self evaluation...should enable settings to reflect on their current strengths and identify next steps which will have a direct impact on children's learning experiences.'

In their efforts to continually improve outcomes for children, Ofsted decided to implement a specific early years self-evaluation tool.

Although the completion of the Self-Evaluation Form is not compulsory, all settings are advised to complete the form. Both the completion of the form or the failure to complete the form can have a very significant effect on the outcome of your inspection.

■ If you do complete your SEF, it is likely to decrease the length of the inspection and helps the inspector

to know what to focus on in the inspection. If completed properly the SEF can ease the process of inspecting for the inspector.

■ If you do not complete your SEF, you will more than likely be asked why and will need a good reason as to why it has not be completed.

■ Failure to complete the form could also mean that your inspection will be longer and more searching. The self-evaluation criteria is likely to be graded lower, although the inspector will check to see what other methods of self-evaluation have been implemented.

Before tackling the SEF, it is worth spending some time reflecting on your setting and its current self-assessment strategies. Settings where reflective practice occurs regularly will find completion of the SEF a much easier task. For further tips on becoming a reflective practitioner please see the previous chapter.

Managers and leaders in settings need to consider what is already being done in the setting to evaluate quality and practice, and how good practice is shared throughout the setting.

The basic key questions of self-evaluation are:

■ How are we doing?

■ How do we know?

■ What are we going to do now?

Involving all staff in the process of self-evaluation will produce higher standards and a sense of ownership over the process of continual development. It is worth remembering that self evaluation only works where individuals within a setting are committed to ensuring high standards and are able to look objectively at practice.

All practitioners need to be aware of what the priorities for improvement are as identified in the SEF, and their role in the ongoing process of working towards improvement. As the SEF is a working document which plays an important role in the development of the setting, please bear in mind that Ofsted will look to validate the statements in your SEF by questioning all staff, whether they are new-starters or not. It is essential then that the setting's SEF is included in the induction process so that all new members of staff are aware the setting's objectives.

Using reflective practice as part of your self-assessment process within the setting will greatly help and support completion of the Self-Evaluation Form. When you first look at the SEF it may look like a daunting task to complete it, but break it down section by section and setting yourself small completion steps can make it seem much more manageable.

The Self-Evaluation Form – what you need to know

Practicalities

- The SEF can be completed online and Ofsted recommend that you use this method.

- You can update your SEF online as often as you like, probably termly, but it should be updated no less than once a year.

- An annually updated hard copy needs to be sent to Ofsted.

- You need a copy of the SEF in the setting at all times ready for the inspector.

- To complete the online form you will need an Ofsted Security Token (OST), which is a unique password, and the guidelines on how to complete the online form. If you have not received an OST you need to contact Ofsted (08456 404043) quoting your Unique Reference Number (www.ofsted.gov.uk).

HINT: Around two days before your inspection, your online SEF will most likely be frozen. This will give you a warning that the inspector is on the way!

Tips for completing the SEF

- Start with the section you find easiest to complete to give yourself a boost, then progress gradually to completing all of the form.

- Make your statements clear and concise and add evidence to back up your statements e.g. refer to policies, planning, observations, records etc., and have these to hand for the inspector to review.

- Use bullet points rather than lengthy paragraphs.

- Try and convey as full a picture as possible of your setting.

- Use a dictionary if you're unsure of a correct spelling. To use a spell check you will need to cut and paste into a word document, as there is no spell check with the online form.

- Ensure you use appropriate terminology and language and avoid jargon and slang.

- Use the Ofsted guidance notes.

- Even though inclusion will be graded separately, it is important to reinforce it throughout the whole SEF.

How to grade yourself

- Be honest, if you feel your provision and/or practice in a specific area is 'outstanding' say so and why.

- Even if you grade yourself as 'outstanding', you still need to identify areas for improvement and what you are hoping to do to make it even better.

- Ofsted will look at how their judgment compares to yours and in doing so will be evaluating your judgements and ability to self evaluate.

The self-evaluation form is broken down into three parts.

These parts are:

Part A

This part covers the setting details and views of those who use the setting. It details the characteristics of your setting and the background of the children. It also asks you to seek the views of all those who use your setting and how you use these views to improve the quality of the provision.

Part B

This covers the evaluation of the outcomes for children and should help you think about and assess your provision. You should answer the questions by taking account of the welfare, learning and development requirements and statutory guidance set out in the EYFS framework.

You should think carefully about any changes and improvements you have made since your most recent inspection. In the text boxes you should describe briefly what you think is working best and describe any plans you have to further improve provision.

Prepare to show Ofsted any evidence you have that supports what you are saying e.g. photographs, documents, risk assessment. These should then be available for the inspector when they visit.

RAG rating

The R in RAG stands for red, the A amber and the G green. This is a simply easily understood way of grading settings and being able to access the grading at a glance. The grading will of course be evidence based.

Most local authorities use a RAG rating to score how settings are doing. During inspection Ofsted may inquire about your RAG rating and it is advisable if you know it to record it on your SEF. The settings may be RAG rated at every visit or through annual dialogue or after an initiative involving the setting.

Preparing for inspection

NOTIFICATION OF INSPECTION

- You will receive a phone call around midday the day before the inspection.
- It will be a short, focused call regarding practical issues.

Ofsted will still inspect without notice if there is a concern.

As we reflect more and more on our practice, less and less specific preparation will be required for an Ofsted inspection – as the idea is that 'we should always be ready'. When considering preparation for an Ofsted inspection, we're not talking about the stereotypical image of the caretaker painting the walls two minutes before the inspector is due to arrive. In this chapter we are looking more broadly at what practitioners need to do to prepare for inspection, both physically and mentally, because readiness can't just be pulled out of the bag on the day. A knock on the door by the Ofsted inspector should be a welcome visit that isn't going to phase any of the practitioners in the setting because they are all prepared and equipped with the knowledge, understanding and strategies to cope.

As previously mentioned, in preparation for inspection you need to ensure that your SEF is completed competently, accurately and that it is up to date. It isn't compulsory, but it is strongly recommended that you have it filled in. Not having done so could adversely affect the outcome of the inspection,

so don't delay, guidance is given in this book to help you complete it. If you haven't completed the form before the inspection, you may be asked to do it on the day and this can cause anxiety and in the rush you could miss vital points, it simply isn't possible to fill it in properly under these conditions. Make sure that you have a hard copy on hand for yourself to refer to during the inspection.

As you update your SEF, be certain to send the updates to Ofsted – this is easy to do online – so that they always have current and relevant information. The inspector will read your SEF before visiting your setting (remember, the online version of the SEF may be frozen approximately two days before the inspection giving you clear indication that you are about to be inspected – but this is NOT a guarantee).

When starting the SEF you need to be organised and share the task of completing it between the entire staff team. Effective teamwork is an essential component in any setting. Without effective teamwork, a setting cannot function properly and maintain standards. The inspector will be very experienced in looking for and identifying signs that show teamwork is either effective or ineffective in the setting. The sense of teamwork in a setting reflects the culture and ethos. Leaders and managers in settings can use the following checklist to

help gain an insight into the sense of teamwork established in different rooms and/or the setting as a whole.

Improvement

The Ofsted inspector will probably take points from the SEF to concentrate on during the visit – although this won't necessarily be the entire focus of the visit – but it does mean that information needs to be accurate and an honest reflection – this is no time for modesty! It is also a time to think of moving your practice forward in a positive way and not seeing problems as obstacles or barriers to improvement, but as challenges to overcome. But don't panic – nothing is perfect straight away and the inspector is not looking for perfection, but looking that you are moving forwards and trying to improve all the time. Even if you judge yourself to be outstanding

Paperwork and systems checklist

Ensuring all of the below are in place will help maintain high quality standards and practice and therefore impact positively on your inspection outcome.

☐ Year plan of appraisals, supervisions and staff observations.

☐ Evaluated staff records with clear and accurate performance records.

☐ Staff meeting yearly plan, to include any information on reviews, file kept of agendas, minutes and actions with clear follow ups, include in file the same for room meetings.

☐ Accident and incident forms in folder with monthly divider, with analysis sheet at the front of each month.

☐ Cover sheet for recruitment indicating reference checks, DBS, 5-year employment record check etc.

☐ Clear overview of professional development linking to reviews,

both of the individual and nursery as a whole.

☐ Targeted plan of when core training needs to be updated.

☐ Overview of 2-year-old progress checks when they were completed, parent seen, manager seen and any targets.

☐ A clear and specific action plan as well as the SEF, including how and when staff and parents contribute.

☐ DBS records clear and to include date to renew, date of issue, number and the name of the agency issuing the check.

☐ Indication within policies and procedures of any amendments, with follow through of how staff are informed, if relevant.

☐ System for management's daily check of registers.

☐ Record detailing when planning and profiles are reviewed and any necessary actions.

☐ Records of how links are established and maintained with schools children may move on to and other settings they may attend.

☐ Clear and accurate cohort analysis with evaluation of that analysis.

☐ Individual room/enabling environment reviews suggesting changes to improve practice/ meet children's needs.

☐ Annual staff suitability check.

☐ First Aid certificates.

they will want to see how you intend to improve even further. A positive outcome of having an accurately completed SEF could be that the inspector may not check out everything that you do and it may shorten the inspection.

Not only do you need to complete your SEF but also get to know your SEF: be aware of, and have a working knowledge of, what actions are being taken, exactly what progress has been made, where your strengths are and where more work is required. It is important that the whole team is involved in this and not just the person responsible for completing the SEF.

If your setting is taking part in any kind of quality assurance award, it is useful to have the relevant information for that to hand also. Ofsted will be interested to see any completed or current modules

with development plans and evidence of the impact these schemes have had on your practice and experiences for the children within the setting. If you have any certificates or plaques for quality assurance awards or training these need to be displayed, as they evidence continued professional development and good practice.

Now we need to think of the more practical things. Can the inspectors find your setting easily? Is the address and phone number up-to-date with Ofsted and are postcodes accurate for your building? This is especially important if the inspectors are using a satellite navigation system to find you.

If you are a pre-school or day care setting, are you clearly advertised and signposted? Are car parking places nearby and easy to find? If the answer

to these two questions is no, is there anything that you can do about it? There is nothing more stress-inducing than not being able to find your way somewhere, then not being able to park the car, not having the right change for the meter and then having a long walk laden down with bags – you really don't want your inspector to arrive to inspect you facing these sorts of conditions. It may be that all you can do is inform them before the visit where they will need to park and if they will need money and how much etc.

Consider the access to your building; this needs to be easy to use for all people including those with additional needs, such as a wheelchair. Can the inspector find where to get in? Is there an efficient way of the door being answered at all times including before the session begins?

Child-centred learning

With every action that you take, it is important to always ensure that the children are at the heart of all that happens. You need to ask yourself how you put children at the centre of your practice and be able to demonstrate this to the inspector. So, for example if through peer observations you decided that your setting's welcome was poor and you decided to change it, you need to put the child at the heart and think 'what would make this a better experience for all the children?'. The next step is to involve the children and their parents and carers by asking for their opinions and valuing them, in this way they will then be far more supportive in implementing any change. Through peer observation you may realise that a particular member of staff does something especially well and may therefore decide to all use that method of practice throughout the setting.

At all times you need to ensure that your environment is safe and stimulating for children to learn and develop and to make any changes that are necessary. Use the skills you have learnt during

reflective practice to assess this, asking yourself relevant questions such as: are there defined areas of learning? Is it bright and airy? Am I an effective practitioner, setting activities up in an inviting manner? Be aware that you need to have robust systems in place for risk assessments, equipment maintenance and safety checks.

It is vital to read through your last inspection as a whole team to address any outstanding issues and simply to remind yourselves of its content. Try not to take the previous report too personally or as criticism, if you can look at it more in terms of guidance for improvement you are more likely to have an open mind when making those improvements. Just because this is Ofsted it doesn't mean that the judgements are always accurate, so you need to consider them carefully and dispassionately and then act accordingly. It is vitally important that you have completed any actions from the previous Ofsted inspection. If you haven't then you need to be able to justify why this is the case.

When you look at the last report it is also a good time to reflect on all the

improvements that you have made, however sometimes in the rush to improve certain areas it is easy to lose sight of the good you were already doing so this is a good time to make sure you haven't let some areas of good practice slide.

Policies and plans

Your polices need to be always up-to-date, reviewed and in order. Best practice is to ensure that these are read and signed by each member of staff and committee members as proof that they have read them.

It is also good to have enabled staff to contribute to policies in order to give them a sense of ownership. This can of course be a lengthy process, but you could consider one or two policies a month over the course of an academic year. Guidance on writing policies and the requirements of individual policies can be obtained from your local Early Years and Childcare Service or from the Pre-school Learning Alliance. Of course, all policies are important, but some details are more vital so pay particular attention that everyone is aware of the safeguarding children policy and those relating to staff conduct.

It's also important that parents/carers are aware of policies and are able to access them – could you include a policy of the month on your newsletters for example to ensure staff and parents have a working knowledge of practice policies?

Be sure that your planning is up-to-date – it's good for it to be annotated with changes made in response to children, that's completely what the inspectors will want to see, but make sure this can be evidenced in your observations.

Talk to the staff – staff are likely to be anxious of inspections particularly if this is their first one or if they have had a bad experience of being inspected.

It's best for staff to be prepared, so brief them with likely scenarios and empower them with responses. The inspector will speak to all staff members so it is important to help them to understand the way questions may be posed and the jargon that may be used. However, most important is to reassure staff of your faith in them and in their good practice so that they can relax and are able to perform to their best ability. This can be achieved through in-house training, constant communication via staff meetings, making sure all staff have access to and are supported during training so that they are well informed and knowledgeable on all aspects of their role.

Have you got an operational plan or a wish list? If so, consult it in preparation for inspection – are there any wishes that you could grant yourself? The feel-good factor of saying we've been able to develop our outdoor play recently by buying x, y or z is worth its weight in gold.

Are you part of a quality assurance scheme? Ofsted suggest that being part of such a scheme is not a guarantee of a good outcome but it is likely to have improved your practice in response to its questions, and completed modules are helpful evidence for the inspector. It is estimated that somewhere in the region of 85% of pre-school settings on a quality assurance scheme receive outstanding Ofsted judgements (www.ofsted.gov.uk).

Ofsted will consider your partnership with parents/carers – it is important that you do this too. Try to think of imaginative ways of sharing information with all parents/carers and enhancing your relationship with them so that they are not only informed but are able to become engaged in the setting – it is proven that parents/carers involved in this early stage of their child's education will be more likely to stay involved in later stages of their education. Something that is often overlooked in

On page 12 the checklist can help you ensure that your paperwork and systems are in place ready for inspection. On page 27 is an example form of how to record any training undertaken by staff and on page 28 a suggested training matrix to track at a glance the qualifications and training of all staff.

preparation for an inspection is whether your setting is culturally aware. One excuse often proffered for not being is 'we don't have any children from that culture here'. However, it is even more important to reflect all members of a diverse society for children who aren't going to have personal experiences of them so that they don't form prejudices and stereotypical viewpoints. Your inclusion practices are the golden thread that you will notice run through all of the SEF questions, therefore it is something to consider extremely carefully and to be transparent about.

Continued professional development is a phrase on all of our minds. Make sure you are aware of all staff training needs and training already undertaken.

SAFEGUARDING

The inspector may not look at all your policies but must look at Safeguarding. The inspector will consider how children are kept safe and protected. There is no grading but it will be commented on under leadership and management.

For this you may need a training matrix which is included in this book. You will want to have a system in place whereby training is cascaded perhaps during staff meetings, or by a simple form that staff fill in when they have been on courses saying what they learnt and how it affected their practice – this can be displayed on the staff notice board for all to read, again a cascade form is included in this book.

This chapter links closely with the chapter on first impressions and it would be wise to go through that to make sure you have everything in place. We've talked a lot about implementing change, but be careful against making change just for the sake of it, if something is good and working well then leave it alone and give yourselves a pat on the back. It is just as important for the whole team to celebrate good practice and achievements as it is to be aware of areas in need of improvement.

The Prevent Duty

This is a duty for you to be aware of and act on any attempts at radicalisation. It is part of the safe guarding duty and staff should be trained on how to recognise radicalisation and what to do if they suspect it. If your setting does not meet these requirements it is likely that funding will be withheld.

In different areas the risk of radicalisation will vary and can change very quickly. Managers and leaders must ensure that all staff are aware of radicalisation, act on suspicions, and communicate and promote the importance of this duty.

The Prevent duty is a move first published in 2011 in order to reduce the threat of terrorism to the UK and to stop people from becoming terrorists or supporting terrorism. In 2015 it was made implicit that funded nurseries and early years settings comply with the prevent duty. The prevent duty simply reinforces existing rules to keep children safe and free from the risks of extremism and terrorism.

From PREVENT DUTY GUIDANCE IN ENGLAND AND WALES (HM Government 2015)

60. Early years providers serve arguably the most vulnerable and impressionable members of society. The Early Years Foundation Stage (EYFS) accordingly places clear duties on providers to keep children safe and promote their welfare. It makes clear that to protect children in their care, providers must be alert to any safeguarding and child protection issues in the child's life at home or elsewhere (paragraph 3.4 EYFS). Early years providers must take action to protect children from harm and should be alert to harmful behaviour by other adults in the child's life.

61. Early years providers already focus on children's personal, social and emotional development The Early Years Foundation Stage framework supports early years providers to do this in an age appropriate way, through ensuring children learn right from wrong, mix and share

with other children and value other's views, know about similarities and differences between themselves and others, and challenge negative attitudes and stereotypes.

Education and childcare specified authorities

65. The education and childcare specified authorities in Schedule 6 to the Act are as follows:

- the proprietors of maintained schools, non maintained special schools, maintained nursery schools, independent schools (including academies and free schools) and alternative provision academies
- pupil referral units
- registered early years childcare providers
- registered later years childcare providers
- providers of holiday schemes for disabled children
- persons exercising local authority functions under a direction of the Secretary of State when the local authority is performing inadequately; and
- persons authorised by virtue of an order made under section 70 of the Deregulation and Contracting Out Act 1994 to exercise a function specified in Schedule 36A to the Education Act 1996.

66. In fulfilling the new duty, we would expect the specified authorities listed above to demonstrate activity in the following areas.

Risk assessment

67. Specified authorities are expected to assess the risk of children being drawn into terrorism, including support for extremist ideas that are part of terrorist ideology. This should be based on an understanding, shared with partners, of the potential risk in the local area.

68. Specified authorities will need to demonstrate that they are protecting children and young people from being drawn into terrorism by having robust safeguarding policies in place to identify children at risk, and intervening as appropriate. Institutions will need to consider the level of risk to identify the most appropriate referral, which could include Channel or Children's Social Care, for example. These policies should set out clear protocols for ensuring that any visiting speakers – whether invited by staff or by children themselves –are suitable and appropriately supervised.

Working in partnership

69. In England, governing bodies and proprietors of all schools and registered childcare providers should ensure that their safeguarding arrangements take into account the policies and procedures of the Local Safeguarding Children Board (LSCB).

75. Early education funding regulations in England have been amended to ensure that providers who fail to promote the fundamental British values of democracy, the rule of law, individual liberty and mutual respect and tolerance for those with different faiths and beliefs do not receive funding from local authorities for the free early years entitlement.

76. Ofsted's current inspection framework for early years provision reflects the requirements in the Statutory Framework for the Early Years Foundation Stage

British Values

British Values is not about having Union Jacks displayed in your setting, it is about a core set of principles which underpin the workings of our society as a nation. Our role in early

years is to break it down to a level which the children can understand and is meaningful to them and provide a foundation for developing these ideals.

Below is a description of the four British Values, relating to Early Years from www.foundationyears.org

Democracy: making decisions together

As part of the focus on self-confidence and self-awareness as cited in Personal, Social and Emotional Development:

- Managers and staff can encourage children to see their role in the bigger picture, encouraging children to know their views count, value each other's views and values and talk about their feelings, for example when they do or do not need help. When appropriate demonstrate democracy in action, for example, children sharing views on what the theme of their role play area could be with a show of hands.

- Staff can support the decisions that children make and provide activities that involve turn-taking, sharing and collaboration. Children should be given opportunities to develop enquiring minds in an atmosphere where questions are valued.

Rule of law: understanding rules matter as cited in Personal, Social and Emotional Development and as part of the focus on managing feelings and behaviour:

- Staff can ensure that children understand their own and others' behaviour and its consequences, and learn to distinguish right from wrong.

- Staff can collaborate with children to create the rules and the codes of behaviour, for example, to agree the rules about tidying up and ensure that all children understand rules apply to everyone.

Individual liberty: freedom for all

As part of the focus on self-confidence and self-awareness and people and communities as cited in Personal, Social and Emotional Development and Understanding the World:

■ Children should develop a positive sense of themselves. Staff can provide opportunities for children to develop their self-knowledge, self-esteem and increase their confidence in their own abilities, for example through allowing children to take risks on an obstacle course, mixing colours, talking about their experiences and learning.

■ Staff should encourage a range of experiences that allow children to explore the language of feelings and responsibility, reflect on their differences and understand we are free to have different opinions, for example in a small group discuss what they feel about transferring into Reception Class.

Mutual respect and tolerance: treat others as you want to be treated

As part of the focus on people and communities, managing feelings and behaviour and making relationships as cited in Personal, Social and Emotional Development and Understanding the World:

■ Managers and leaders should create an ethos of inclusivity and tolerance where views, faiths, cultures and races are valued and children are engaged with the wider community.

■ Children should acquire a tolerance and appreciation of and respect for their own and other cultures; know about similarities and differences between themselves and others and among families, faiths, communities, cultures

and traditions and share and discuss practices, celebrations and experiences.

■ Staff should encourage and explain the importance of tolerant behaviours such as sharing and respecting other's opinions.

■ Staff should promote diverse attitudes and challenge stereotypes, for example, sharing stories that reflect and value the diversity of children's experiences and providing resources and activities that challenge gender, cultural and racial stereotyping.

From www.foundationyears.org.uk

How might you see British Values in your setting?

Each value needs to be embedded and reflected in a variety of ways.

VALUE	HOW IT MIGHT BE SEEN IN THE SETTING	EVIDENCE FROM YOUR SETTING	IMPROVEMENT
Democracy: Making decisions together	■ Child initiated activity ■ Making choices ■ Snack time choice ■ Choosing a story ■ Do I want to be inside or outside? ■ Selecting activities ■ Playing group games ■ Contributing to planning		
Rule of Law	■ Helping children to develop self control ■ Considering other people's feelings ■ Children to contribute to a 'charter' 'we use kind hands', 'we walk inside' etc ■ Tidying up ■ Giving children strategies to deal with negative emotions ■ Positive reinforcement and specific praise		
Individual liberty: freedom for all	■ Positive self esteem ■ Encouraging children to have their own ideas ■ Promoting independence and self help skills ■ Learning to respect each other and our differences ■ Allowing children to take risks		
Mutual respect and tolerance: treat others as you want to be treated	■ Celebrating different festivals ■ Taking part in the local community ■ Charity events ■ Being kind to each other ■ Playing alongside each other		

For Quality of Teaching

Ofsted will not specify a particular method of teaching but are looking for good practice over all. The checklist will help you recognise evidence of examples of quality teaching in your setting.

Teaching example	Evidence
Interaction with children during child initiated activity and play	
Interaction with children during planned adult led activities	
Communicating and modelling language	
Showing, demonstrating and explaining	
Exploring ideas, encouraging and questioning	
Recalling	
Providing narrative for what they are doing	
Facilitating and setting challenges	
Assessment of what children know, understand and can do	
Children's interests, dispositions to learn (characteristics of effective learning)	

It is key to be able to identify how practitioners use information to plan children's next steps in learning and monitor their progress.

Quality Improvement Plan

Since November 2013, Ofsted inspectors have been required to also take into account the bigger picture of the setting. This is added to the evidence gathered during the inspection. The bigger picture includes previous Ofsted gradings and reports. It will also mean considering the present state and future plans for the setting. For this reason it is implicitly important to have completed any actions required of previous Ofsted inspections and to have a Quality Improvement Plan for

the setting. The history and information held on the setting will be taken into account – for example, complaints and responses to complaints.

The inspector must be rigorous and thorough in evaluating how past events have impacted on the setting and how well they continue to meet the needs of children. This makes it vital that Ofsted have been informed if anything out of the ordinary has occurred, and if anything unusual happens on the day of

inspection that you make the inspector aware that this does not usually happen. These will be used to by the inspector to make an overall judgement. It is always useful to have a folder of documents of improvements you have made and intend to make ready to show to the inspector. During inspection, inspectors must take into account the context of the setting – for example, how long the children have been attending the setting, their ages and stages of development.

Aim							
	Resources	How to achieve	By who	Due date	Date completed	Impact	Benefits to children
Action 1							
Action 2							
Action 3							
Action 4							
Action 5							
Action 6							

The effectiveness of leadership and management of the early years provision

OUTSTANDING		
DESCRIPTOR	**EVIDENCE**	**DEVELOPMENT**
The pursuit of excellence in all the setting's activities is demonstrated by an uncompromising, highly successful drive to improve achievement or maintain the highest levels of achievement for all children.		
Incisive evaluation of the impact of staff's practice leads to rigorous performance management, supervision and highly focused professional development. As a result, teaching is highly effective or improving rapidly.		
Leaders and managers actively seek, evaluate and act on the views of parents, staff and children to drive continual improvement.		
Highly effective monitoring identifies where children may be slow to develop key skills so that specific programmes of support are implemented to help them catch up. Gaps in achievement between different groups of children, especially those for whom the setting receives additional funding are negligible or closing.		
The provider has excellent knowledge of the requirements of the Early Years Foundation Stage, and implements them highly effectively.		
Leaders' deep understanding of the curriculum and how to apply it to meet the needs and interests of children results in all staff planning highly effective activities. As a result, children are exceptionally well prepared to move on, including, where appropriate, to school.		
Leaders set high standards for children's behaviour at all times. Exemplary relationships between staff provide an excellent model for children's behaviour towards each other.		
Highly effective partnership working leads to improvement in provision and outcomes for children and their families.		
The promotion of equality, diversity and British values is at the heart of the setting's work. It is demonstrated through all its practices, including tackling any instances of discrimination and being alert to potential risks from radicalisation and extremisim.		
Safeguarding and welfare meet statutory requirements. Leaders and managers have created a culture of vigilance where children's welfare is actively promoted. Children are listened to and feel safe. Staff are trained to identify and support children who may be at risk of neglect or abuse and they report any concerns. Work with partner agencies to safeguard children's welfare is effective.		

The effectiveness of leadership and management of the early years provision

GOOD		EVIDENCE	DEVELOPMENT
DESCRIPTOR			
Leaders and managers are ambitious and communicate high expectations to all. Self-evaluation is accurate and includes the views of parents, staff and children. Actions taken by leaders to improve the quality of provision, as required by the Early Years Foundation Stage, are carefully planned and effective.			
An effective well established programme of professional development helps practitioners to improve their knowledge, understanding and practice. Through effective systems for supervision and performance, management and practitioners are monitored regularly and under performance tackled swiftly. As a result, teaching is consistently strong or improving steadily.			
Leaders ensure that the curriculum provides a broad range of interesting and demanding experiences that help children to make progress towards reaching the early learning goals. As a result, children are well prepared to move on, including where appropriate to school.			
Monitoring ensures that individual children or groups of children who have identified needs are targeted and appropriate interventions are secured so that children receive the support they need, including through effective partnerships with external agencies and other providers.			
Relationships between staff provide a good model from which children learn about how to behave towards others. Leaders have high expectations for consistently good behaviour.			
Additional funding for disadvantaged children is used effectively to narrow gaps in outcomes. Partnerships with local providers are leading to improvements in provision and outcomes for children in the setting.			
Leaders and managers actively promote equality, diversity and British values through all policies and practice. They tackle instances of discrimination effectively.			
Safeguarding is effective and the setting meets statutory requirements. The provider ensures that staff have a good understanding of how to manage, and minimise, risks for children without limiting opportunities for their development. Safeguarding and child protection policies and procedures, including safer recruitment, are implemented consistently, practice is reviewed regularly and clearly evaluated.			

Teaching, learning and assessment

OUTSTANDING		
DESCRIPTOR	**EVIDENCE**	**DEVELOPMENT**
All practitioners have very high expectations of what each child can achieve, including the most able and the most disadvantaged.		
Teaching is consistently of a very high quality, inspirational and worthy of dissemination to others; it is highly responsive to children's needs.		
Practitioners use their expert knowledge of the areas of learning and deep understanding of how children learn to provide rich, varied and imaginative experiences that enthuse, engage and motivate children to learn.		
Accurate assessment, including through high quality observations, is rigorous and sharply focused and includes all those involved in the child's learning and development. Where appropriate, children are involved in the process. Information from assessment is used to secure timely interventions and support, based on a comprehensive knowledge of the child and their family.		
Provision across all areas of learning is planned meticulously and based on regular and precise assessments of children's achievement so that every child undertakes highly challenging activities.		
Highly successful strategies engage parents, including those from different groups, in their children's learning, both in the setting and at home.		
Practitioners provide an exceptional range of resources and activities that reflect and value the diversity of children's experiences. They actively challenge gender, cultural and racial stereotyping and help children gain an understanding of people, families and communities beyond their immediate experience.		
The extremely sharp focus on helping children to acquire communication and language skills, and on supporting their physical, personal, social and emotional development, gives children the foundations for future learning.		

Teaching, learning and assessment

GOOD		
DESCRIPTOR	**EVIDENCE**	**DEVELOPMENT**
Practitioners have high expectations of all children based on accurate assessment of children's skills, knowledge and understanding when they join the setting.		
The quality of teaching is consistently strong. Practitioners have a secure knowledge and understanding of how to promote the learning and development of young children and what they can achieve.		
Practitioners complete regular and precise assessments of children's learning that they use to effectively plan suitably challenging activities. They observe carefully, question skilfully and listen perceptively to children during activities in order to re-shape activities and give children explanations that improve their learning.		
Practitioners teach the basics well and support children to learn the communication and language skills and develop the physical, personal, social and emotional skills they need for the next steps in their learning. Where appropriate, early literacy skills and mathematical development are promoted effectively to ensure that children are ready for school.		
The key person system works effectively to engage parents, including those who may be more reluctant to contribute, in their children's learning. Parents contribute to initial assessments of children's starting points on entry and they are kept informed about their children's progress. Parents are encouraged to support and share information about their children's learning and development at home.		
Practitioners provide a wide range of opportunities for children to learn about people and communities beyond their immediate experience. Resources and activities reflect and value the diversity of children's backgrounds and experiences.		

Personal development, behaviour and welfare

OUTSTANDING		
DESCRIPTOR	**EVIDENCE**	**DEVELOPMENT**
The highly stimulating environment and wide range of activities ensure that children are highly motivated and very eager to join in. They consistently show the characteristics of effective learning. They show high levels of curiosity, imagination and concentration. Older children listen intently and are highly responsive to adults and each other.		
Children's health, welfare and well being are significantly enhanced by the vigilant and highly consistent implementation of robust policies, procedures and practice. High standards of care and hygiene practice support the personal care needs of babies and toddlers.		
Practitioners are highly skilled and sensitive in helping children of all ages form secure emotional attachments. This gives children a strong base for developing their independence to explore their world and increases their confidence in their own abilities.		
Children increasingly show high levels of confidence in social situations. They develop a positive sense of themselves and their place in the world. They develop a very good understanding of how to keep themselves safe and how to manage risks and challenges.		
The strong skills of all key persons ensure all children are emotionally well prepared for the next stages in their learning. Practitioners skilfully support children's transitions both within the setting and to other settings and prepare them for the move to school.		
Children demonstrate exceptionally positive behaviour and high levels of self control, cooperation and respect for others that are appropriate for their age. They do not distract others or become distracted themselves.		
Children's welfare and personal development are central to everything practitioners do. They are very effective in supporting children's growing understanding of how to keep themselves safe and healthy.		
Practitioners give children a wide range of experiences that promote understanding of people, families and communities beyond their own. They teach children the language of feelings and give them opportunities to reflect on their differences.		

Personal development, behaviour and welfare

GOOD		
DESCRIPTOR	**EVIDENCE**	**DEVELOPMENT**
Practitioners provide a stimulating, welcoming environment, both indoors and out, that keeps children motivated and interested in a broad range of activities. Children are keen learners who regularly display the characteristics of effective learning. They listen carefully to adults and each other.		
A well established key person system helps children form secure attachments and promotes their well being and independence. Relationships between staff and babies are sensitive, stimulating and responsive.		
Practitioners adhere consistently to agreed strategies to promote good behaviour and regular attendance. They provide clear guidance for children about what is and is not acceptable behaviour.		
Practitioners help children to become independent in managing their own personal needs.		
Key persons ensure children are emotionally well prepared for the next stages in their learning.		
Children's good behaviour shows that they feel safe. They gain an understanding of risk through activities that encourage them to explore their environment.		
Practitioners give clear messages to children about why it is important to have a healthy diet and the need for physical exercise while providing these things within the setting.		
Children are learning to respect and celebrate each other's differences. They develop an understanding of diversity beyond their immediate family experience through a range of activities that teach them effectively about people in the wider world.		

Outcomes for children

OUTSTANDING

DESCRIPTOR	EVIDENCE	DEVELOPMENT
Children make consistently high rates of progress in relation to their starting points and are extremely well prepared for the next stage of their education.		
Almost all children in the provision, including disabled children, those who have special educational needs, those for whom the setting receives additional funding and the most able, are making substantial and sustained progress that leads to outstanding achievement.		
Gaps between the attainment of groups of children in the setting, including those for whom the setting receives additional funding, have closed or are closing rapidly. Any differences between outcomes in different areas of learning are closing.		
Children are highly motivated and very eager to join in. They consistently demonstrate the characteristics of effective learning.		

GOOD

DESCRIPTOR	EVIDENCE	DEVELOPMENT
Children make at least typical progress and most children make progress that is better than typical from their starting points. This includes disabled children, those who have special educational needs, those for whom the setting receives additional funding and the most able.		
Where children's starting points are below those of other children of their age, assessment shows they are improving consistently over a sustained period and the gap is closing. Any gaps between the attainment of groups, including those for whom the setting receives additional funding are closing.		
Children are working comfortably within the range of development typical for their age, taking account of any whose starting points are higher or any disabled children and those with special educational needs.		
Children develop the key skills needed for the next steps in their learning, including, where appropriate, for starting school.		

Cascade from training

Title of course attended	
Date of course attended	
Name(s) of staff attending the course	
General description of content of the course	
Three points for development from the course or ideas gained from the course	1. 2. 3.

Training matrix

Staff name	Qualification – Date gained	DBS – Date and number	First Aid – Date	Appraisal – Date	Supervision – Date	Safe guarding children – Date	Courses requested – identified at appraisal and supervision	Courses attended – Date	Cascade – yes/no – Date

'First impressions count'

The inspectors are professional people who aren't going to be fooled by the veneer of everything on the surface looking superficially good, but the practice being poor. They aren't going to make judgements solely based on their first impressions either, they are professionally far more objective than that.

However, the first impression does influence opinion and can change the feel of a visit. For example, the following statement is taken directly from an Ofsted report: 'It is obvious from the moment the doors open and the children rush in that this is a happy and lively place where learning is fun'.

Inspectors spend most of the day gathering first hand evidence by observing, but the first impressions will always count.

They will start by grading your setting as **Good**, if you exceed that in all areas you will be graded as **Outstanding**. If you fall below you will be graded with the new outcome, **Requires Improvement**. If there are significant weaknesses and breaches of the statutory requirements, you will be graded as **Inadequate**. The inspector will expect consistency – if the leadership and management are weak, the welfare of the children cannot realistically be good.

This chapter aims to explore first impressions and how we can ensure that they are favourable in getting a true reflection and judgement of your setting.

Arrival

Hopefully the Ofsted inspector will have arrived at your door safely, having been informed and signposted of how to gain access to your building. On their walk from car or train to the door they are going to be looking around to see if the setting is inviting and welcoming.

They are going to ring on the doorbell and may have to wait in the foyer for a few minutes, this can be an illuminating experience and one you should try yourself to give a true picture of what it is going to be like. Ask yourself the question: is the foyer warm, welcoming and comfortable? It's worth providing somewhere for parents and carers to sit. Does everyone in your foyer feel at ease and welcome?

Are any information and notices given in an accessible manner to everyone including those with additional needs?

Standing in the foyer of a setting waiting can be a revealing experience. Whether you have to wait often depends on who answers the door, it is then about how long you wait. Are there interesting and informative noticeboards to read? What else can you see and hear? As a visitor I often just stand and listen and wonder what it would be like to be a parent or child in that setting, especially a new parent – do I feel I belong? Or do I feel outside 'the group'? Are parents exchanging information which is sensitive and that really shouldn't be aired in

Try to ensure that the dynamics of your team always remain professional on inspection day. To witness the team working together in a friendly manner with a good rapport will prove to the inspector that you work well together and will be supportive as a team during challenging times. Indicators of good team work are shared goals, respect and friendliness to one another. This is not about being matey it is about being professional and sincere in your approach to your work. The inspector will be experienced in what effective teamwork looks like. Below are some indicators of positive teamwork.

- Does the room appear organised?

- Are the staff communicating verbally, is there also evidence of non verbal communication e.g. message books?

- Are the children happy and on task and are their physical needs being met?

- Do the staff appear to be aware of their role and responsibilities?

- Is there a happy and positive atmosphere?

- Are the displays up to date?

- Is a visual routine displayed?

- Do the children respond to the adults?

- Do the adults respond to the children?

public? Are they chatting about the setting in a positive and encouraging manner?

Am I spoken to or am I ignored? Is there something for me to do whilst I wait or something informative for me to read. The foyer is a hazy area of responsibility but you need to try and create an area that reflects the rest of the setting and shouldn't be overlooked in the whole picture.

It leaves a bad impression if the inspector has to ask for the book to sign in, so when they arrive please remember to show and ask them to sign in using the visitor's book. The visitor's book must have a column for the name, date, time in and out, company and purpose of visit. Also, don't forget to tell the inspector about your emergency procedures and if there are any emergency drills planned for that day and mobile phone policy. Remember to ask for ID and you or the inspector will need to put a sign up at the entrance indicating an inspection is taking place.

Greeting the inspector

The greeting – this can be a tricky one! You're about to be inspected – you're bound to be anxious and possibly more than a little tense – this is true for the whole team – but do try to relax, breath deeply, be friendly and above all be professional! Find the time please to introduce the inspector to the whole team, including any committee members who are present. Do show the inspector where they can put their bag and coat and where the toilets are.

It is likely to be whoever is on the door that day that welcomes the Ofsted inspector so this could be the newest, least trained member of staff. It is worth considering putting something in the staff induction programme of the setting that includes how to behave during Ofsted inspections – including some role play situations as part of the staff observation system, managers need to ask practitioners questions to help prepare them for the inspection.

Your approach to the children in the setting must also reflect normality – try to be the same with the children as you always are, any tension that you're feeling will rub off on them. It is so easy to detect false behaviour – the children will be the first to see through it! You're not going to get an inadequate judgement if the day the inspector comes six children are crying, Johnie and Alice have just bitten each other, the school fish has died and a member of staff is emotional! Unless of course you leave the six children uncomforted, you don't help Johnie and Alice to resolve their dispute amicably, you leave the fish floating in the bowl and you let the member of staff wreak havoc! It's how you handle the situations you're faced with that count and also what caused them in the first place; could reflective practice have identified areas for improvement that would negate these problems? For example, have observations revealed that children are unsettled on arrival and have you and your team discussed ways to improve this situation, e.g. to move straight into free flow play at the beginning of a session?

It is important that all staff are identifiable, this is for children and parents and carers on an everyday level as well as for inspectors. You

can achieve this simply and relatively cheaply by them all wearing name badges, or tabards or the same bright coloured tee-shirts. A named photograph, displayed with staff titles and responsibilities and also training is also a pleasant touch. Not only does being identifiable help everyone know who everyone else is it also demonstrates a sense of pride in your place of work.

Once the inspector has walked through the door, been greeted and signed in, they will no doubt pause and look around the room to get a feel for the place, to get an idea of the general ambiance, this is another chance to make a positive first impression. They will want to see a bright and airy clean room – that doesn't mean there is no paint or water or sand or glitter, those things are meant to be there. It means there aren't five-year-old cobwebs and displays of children's work that are so old that the paper is curled and the season has passed.

We all have our little foibles of what's important to us and the Ofsted inspector is no different. There will be something that they are extra keen on to look at first, however during the course of the visit they will look at everything that they want to. Everyone has something different that will catch their eye in a setting. It could be display boards and how they reflect the setting, or the cleanliness, quite apart from what the staff and children are doing. The first impressions checklist on page 26 will help highlight some of these areas.

A good way to know what the first impression your setting may give, is to try to experience it yourself, or visit other settings to see how their practice is similar or varies from yours. Then identify your own strengths and weaknesses and see where

improvements can be made. You could set up a video to record the beginning of your sessions or simply video around the setting – it's amazing what you will see through this. Or get a fresh pair of eyes in to look for you – it is worth asking your local early years team if they could evaluate some areas for you to provide reassurance. You should network with other local settings and within the team as you may get ideas that you could use. Peer observations with feedback and evaluation at staff meetings will help you to identify areas of strength both individually and as a team, and identify those areas that require development – there is more information on these in the 'Preparing for your inspection' chapter of this book.

If you have a member of staff who is weak, or about whom you may have concerns, inform the inspector and explain how you are managing their performance.

First impressions checklist

What the inspector may look for	Comment	Met	Partly Met	Not Met
Is there a range and variety of activities available that are age/stage appropriate?	Are you sure that activities suit all children in the setting – e.g. no small parts?			
Are activities set out on different levels?	Are there table top, floor, wall activities?			
Do activities encourage exploration and investigation?	Do adults model investigation and exploration?			
Are resources up to date and relevant?	Children need to experience activities relevant to their lives.			
Are all resources fit for purpose?	All pieces present for puzzles, no splinters on wood, all pages of books.			
Is the children's paint fresh?	Is paint stirred and refreshed daily – are there plenty of colours for children to mix?			
Is the playdough fresh?	Do the children make the playdough themselves, is there a choice of colour, texture and tools etc?			
Can children initiate their own play through free choice?	This will be apparent immediately.			
Are resources clearly labelled with words and pictures?	Children first learn to read through looking at pictures and identifying symbols and making representations.			
Are all the staff interacting and engaging with the children?	This can include observing the children.			
Is there a clear learning intention to each activity?	Would every adult present know what you are hoping to get from each activity?			
Are the activities provided exciting?	Ask yourself 'Would I want to play here if I was a child?'.			
Do the children appear to be happy and engaged?	If children are bored they can become frustrated.			
Do children and adults appear to have a sense of pride in this setting?	Is it untidy and cluttered?			
Are there displays of children's work? Are these clearly labelled, perhaps with a child's photo?	Is every child's work included? Are these up to date? Is all the work displayed the children's own or is it done by adults?			
Are displays child height?	Are they bright and colourful?			
Would all children feel that they belong here?	Does each child have their own peg, tray etc?			
Are staff easily identifiable?	Do the staff wear uniforms or name badges?			
If English was not my first language could I access information?	Consider how you make sure that messages are received and understood.			
Is there a visual routine?	This helps children with routine and transitions.			
Have you got key person lists with photographs of the key persons?				
Are areas of learning easily identifiable?	Do children and adults know where to go to do each activity?			
Does the setting smell fresh?				
Do children have free access to drinking water?	It is better to have free flowing water, but be sure that it is fresh every day.			

What the inspector may look for	Comment	Met	Partly Met	Not Met
Are the toilets well stocked with soap, handtowels and toilet paper etc.?	It is best practice to use liquid soap not bars of soap.			
Is there access to natural materials?	It's good to have natural resources indoors and outdoors.			
Are all cultures equally reflected amongst toys, displays etc.?	This is especially important where some cultures are not physically present.			
Is there free flow play indoors and outdoors?	Are staff actively encouraging free flow?			
Are all staff well deployed?	Does every member of staff know what they are doing and why they are doing it?			
Is statutory paperwork displayed? Where?	E.g. Insurance certificate, Ofsted registration etc.			
Is there any evidence of a Quality Improvement Plan?	Do you have a Quality Improvement Plan that you can show the inspector – perhaps you are part of a quality improvement award scheme.			
Would I know what to do in case of emergency in this setting?	Remember to tell every visitor your emergency plan when they arrive.			
Are first aiders identified?	Is there a notice displayed with first aiders names?			
Is there clear evidence of a strong partnership with parents/carers?	This will be evident in parent rotas, the rapport between parents and staff etc.			
Is the building secure?	Make sure any gates etc. are locked.			

Step by step guide to completing your Self-Evaluation Form

Part A: Section 1 – Your setting

This is the only section of the SEF that Ofsted can quote *verbatim* in the report – be sure it is factual and to the point.

You need to state the number of children who use the setting and give a brief description of their ages, genders, social and cultural backgrounds and whether they have learning difficulties and special educational needs.

Here you can list any special features of your setting e.g. participation in a quality assurance scheme.

Questions from page 5 Ofsted SEF guidance	Features to consider	Evidence suggestions
Your building including area and rooms used.	Describe your building – its age and style. List any other users.	
The area your provision is in.	Is it a residential or industrial area, rural or urban?	
Any access to an outdoor space.	Do you have an outdoor area that children can use on a daily free flow basis? If not, what access to outdoor play do you have?	
Access to and within the building – such as a lift, ramp or stairs.	Describe access and give consideration to access for those with additional needs. This must include plans for what you would do should a need arise.	
The days and hours you operate and the maximum number of places available on any one day.		
The number and qualifications of the adults working with the children and any support staff, such as a cook.	List the qualifications of all staff – check with current legislation that levels and percentages are correct.	
Recent training attended or any qualifications gained.	List training taken within the past year including any relevant short courses.	
Difficulties in recruiting and retaining staff.	Describe any problems you may have had in this area.	
Recent or impending reorganisation or change of staff.	Is anyone about to leave or to become qualified? Is there any impending internal promotion?	

Part A: Section 1 continued

Questions from page 5 Ofsted SEF guidance	Features to consider	Evidence suggestions
How your provision is organised including any links to schools or children's centres.		
Any special features of provision.	Any particular methods of teaching?	Forest School

Part A: Section 2 – Views of those who use your setting

Questions from page 6 Ofsted SEF guidance	Features to consider/ reflective questions	Evidence suggestions
How do you know what their views are? Do you ask parents/carers and others to complete a questionnaire about how satisfied they are with the provision, or do you meet with parents/carers to discuss the provision?	Did you issue a questionnaire to ask parents/carers their views? Are parents/carers given an open door access to the setting and an opportunity to air their views? Do you have a questionnaire for new parents/carers as part of the settling-in process? Do you give out the questionnaire annually and an exit questionnaire?	How did you use the information gained from responses to the questionnaire? Have you got examples of changes made as a result? Do you have a summary sheet of key responses? Do you have evidence of dates and times of such meetings and copies of questionnaires? Do you have a summary of responses to questionnaires?
Are parents/carers represented on the management body?	Parents/carers group/pre-school committee.	
How do you know children's views and ideas and those of the staff?	Do you do a review of each session with the children? Do you regularly ask children for their views and ideas of what they would like to do with the provision? Are staff able to express their ideas freely and are these ideas embraced if practically possible? Do you have staff interviews and appraisals to consider their views and ideas?	Children could be given cameras and asked to take photographs of areas they like or dislike about the setting – e.g. outdoor space. What changes have you made in response to those views – show evidence e.g. in the form of an action plan.
How you work with other organisations e.g. if you have any agreed protocols, whether you are part of a QA Scheme or use any other systems or methods to assess what to do, reference to any local authority support and recommendations and examples of feedback you have from other professionals who work with you or children you care for. Examples of any action you have taken to change provision as a result of views of others.	ECERS (Early Childhood Environment Rating Scales) ITERS (Infant Toddler Environment Rating Scales).	NDNA Quality Counts ECERS (Early Childhood Environment Rating Scales) ITERS (Infant Toddler Environment Rating Scales) Annual LA Conversation SEN support Independent consultants.

Part B: The quality and standards of the Early Years provision

The table below will help you to consider the questions on page 7 and 8 of the SEF guidance booklet.

Links can be made to EYFS card 4.4 Areas of Learning and Development and EYFS pages 4 – 12 'Development Matters'. You must be able to show academic progress.

Section 3: Effectiveness of leadership and management

This section refers to pages 7 and 8 of the Ofsted SEF Guidance.
You should evaluate how well your leadership and management activities do the following:

Action	Reflection and Evidence
Create a culture of excellence where children can excel.	
Help your staff improve.	How familiar are you with staff skills and areas for development, how do you support both areas for each member of staff?
	A clear annual plan for appraisals, supervisions and staff observation.
	Clear targets set for the individual and in some instances feeding into the whole setting quality improvement plan.
	Offer opportunities for personal or professional development through training, coaching, mentoring, skill sharing and responsibility.
	Ensure training is targeted using training focus forms and allow practitioners to cascade back what has been learnt.
	An up-to-date training matrix.
	Regular staff meetings, with clear minutes kept which identify any actions agreed.
Evaluate the quality of your provision, and make successful improvements based on this evaluation.	How do you review quality throughout your provision?
	Do you undertake
	■ Room observations
	■ Quality/learning and development audits
	■ Safeguarding audits
	■ Welfare audits
	■ Use the evaluation from the cohort progress tracker to inform
	In addition, do you use information from parent questionnaires, feedback from staff and reviews of practice and procedure that might be discussed in staff meetings.
	Have an up-to-date and robust Quality Improvement Plan, with clear targets, which are broken down to identify how they will be achieved and identify expected impact of improvements and track the actual impact of these improvements.

Action	Reflection and Evidence
Provide a learning environment, programme and curriculum that is suitably broad, and meets the needs and interests of the children.	A clear system for monitoring observation, assessment and planning. Ensuring that all staff understand the process and that individual needs are met. Do you track the range of observations undertaken? How you meet the needs of children with additional needs. The effectiveness of the SENCO in the setting. Reviews of the provision both indoors and outdoors ensuring that there is depth and breadth across the 7 areas.
Support all children so that they get a good start and are ready for the next stage in their learning.	How do you use information from children's starting points assessment? How do you review the cohort analysis and tackle any gaps in achievement, through targeted support or reviewing provision. How do you identify how to use EYPP funding and how do you monitor the impact on the child/ren of that additional funding. This should be logged identifying expected impact and actual impact. How do you support transitions? What links do you have with local schools? How do you prepare children for starting school?
Promote equality and diversity, promote British values and tackle poor behaviour, including bullying.	Equal opportunities policy. Behaviour policy. Do you ensure that all adults and children are included and that unacceptable behaviour and attitudes are challenged? Do you log any incidents of discrimination? What examples do you have as to how British values are promoted and embedded in everyday practice?
Meet the statutory requirements of the EYFS and other government requirements.	Policies and procedures. Compliance paperwork. EYPP funding tracking. 2 year old integrated review.
Meet requirements to make sure that all children are safe, and protected from radicalisation and extremism.	Have you attended safer recruitment training? Pre-employment checklist, including 5 year employment history tracking. Annual staff suitability check. Safeguarding policies. Current enhanced DBS checks. Risk assessments.
Support partnership working with parents and agencies to support children in your setting.	Is there an open door policy whereby parents can easily approach staff? What methods do you use to help parents to support their children's development at home? Do you have a policy and procedure to support parents with transitions of their children? Are 'All About Me' forms completed with key person, parents and children? Are parents made aware of your policies and procedures? If so, how? Do parents have the opportunity to be involved in the writing of policies? How do you liaise with other providers, other professionals who may work with a child and schools to ease transitions and inform parents?

Part B: Section 3 continued

Action	Reflection and Evidence
Support partnership working with parents and agencies to support children in your setting.	Do you have regular consultation meetings?
	Do you complete daily or weekly home setting diaries?
	Do you give parents free access to observations on their children?
	Do you hold workshops for parents and carers to understand child development?
	Do you explain to parents/carers the stage of development a child is at?
	Do you practise safety routines regularly, recording and evaluating their outcomes?
	Do you have effective systems to ensure that ratios are kept at all times not only throughout the setting but in individual rooms?
	Do you ensure that all equipment is safe and regularly check this?
	Do you evaluate your accident and incident books to consider if there are improvements that you can make to lessen these?

Part B: Section 4 – Quality of teaching, learning and assessment

This section refers to pages 8 and 9 of the Ofsted SEF Guidance. You should evaluate how well you do the following:

Action	Reflection and Evidence
Understand the age group you work with and if you have high enough expectations of each child.	How do practitioners differentiate their planning? Does planning show how children's individual needs are met? Is information from observations reflected in planning? Are practitioners skilled at extending learning in activities to develop understanding skills and move them on to another level? Give examples. During the process of staff/room observations, does the manager/leader question practitioners about children's learning and how it might be extended? Is planning evaluated, to reflect on what children learnt and how something could be improved/developed? Are children enabled to follow their own ideas in activities to demonstrate their understanding and skills and follow through an idea or a thought? Give examples.
Use assessment information to understand children's current level of development, and how you use this to plan their learning over time.	Do you carry out termly progress summary reports, to enable practitioners to reflect on where their key children are at and then being able to identify where they need to go next? Learning journeys and assessment records are part of the evidence. If next steps are identified from observations, is this reflected in provision/fed into planning? A clear observation, assessment and planning cycle will evidence and demonstrate this in practice.
Support children to develop the characteristics of effective learning.	Have practitioners had training on the characteristics of effective learning? Do you carry out observations/environment audits to identify the opportunities available to the children that enable the characteristics of effective learning? Are the characteristics of effective learning reflected in your observation analysis and your planning?
Work in partnership with parents and carers to support each child's learning, in and out of the provision.	Do you invite parents to contribute to children's assessments? Do you encourage them to share the children's achievements from home? What strategies and systems do you have in place to support parents to support their children's learning and development at home? Do you have story bags and or library books they take home? Do you have any activity suggestion cards or activity packs that they can use with their children? How do you evaluate this involvement? Do you ask for parent feedback?
Promote equality and diversity through teaching.	Are practitioners skilled at identifying children who need extra support? Both less able and more able? How does the SENCO support practitioners? How do you use information from cohort progress analysis that identifies gaps between different groups to improve and develop opportunities?

Part B: Section 5 – Personal development, behaviour and welfare

This section refers to page 9 of the Ofsted SEF Guidance. You should evaluate how well you do the following:

Action	Reflection and Evidence
Secure emotional attachments with their key person.	How do you allocate key people?
	Does each child have a named second key person, if their first key person is absent?
	Does your settling in process enable children (especially in baby rooms) to spend one to one time with their key person?
	Do you have a key person board with photos?
	In the child's profile is there an introduction all about me, about the key person?
	For very young children, do you follow routines from home?
	Do children know who their key person is?
	Does the key person complete their key children's assessments?
	How does the key person build a relationship with the child's family?
	Do children attend regularly? If a child has periods of absence what action do you take?
Learn to behave and develop good relationships with their peers.	Is your behaviour policy clear and appropriate?
	Is the approach to behaviour for each individual child consistent and reflective of their development?
	What strategies do you use to promote positive behaviour?
	Do you create an atmosphere and an environment where children will want to learn and be able to engage and concentrate? How do you feel you enable this to happen?
	Do you provide activities that arouse curiosity and anticipation?
	Are children encouraged by good example to value what others say – e.g.being quiet whilst others are speaking.
	Are you positive and good role models – are adults within the team friendly towards each other? How do you ensure this happens?
	Do you use discussion, circle time, puppets and story time to help children understand the qualities of friendship and do you encourage the language of friendship? Give examples.
	Do you help children resolve their differences with empathy and sensitivity? Give examples.
	Can children sometimes choose who they sit next to e.g. for snack or lunch time?
	Are children enabled to engage in free flow play and make choices and decisions about their play and activities?
	Are practitioners aware of the social stages of development in play, how is this reflected in practice?
Keep themselves healthy and safe.	What is your medicine policy?
	What hygiene routines do you have?
	Do you talk to children about the spread of infection and how to reduce this?
	Do you have colour coded placemats with the children's photo on and identifying any dietary needs/requirements?
	You should have up-to-date information from parents or carers of child's medical conditions, allergies, special diet etc.

Part B: Section 5 continued

Action	Reflection and Evidence
Keep themselves healthy and safe.	How well do you teach children to be active and understand the benefits of physical activity? Give examples.
	Understand and adopt healthy habits? Give examples.
	Make healthy choices about what to eat and drink.
	Copy of healthy eating policy. This is about more than only having fruit at snack time, it is about giving children healthy options and informed choices for a balanced diet and including foods from different cultures.
	Menu.
	Pictorial instructions for hand washing and nose blowing etc.
	Copy of food hygiene certificates.
	Named person responsible for health and safety.
Become self-aware and confident learners.	How do you support children's self help skills and independence, both through play and activities and in looking after their own needs? What impact does this have on the children's confidence?
	Can children lead their own learning, by discovering and exploring the environment, making connections and becoming aware of their own skills.
	How can children explore risk?
	How do you prepare children to start school in relation to their confidence and self esteem?

Part B: Section 6 – Outcomes for children

This section refers to pages 9 and 10 of the Ofsted SEF Guidance.
You should evaluate how well you do the following:

Action	Reflection and Evidence
Identify children's starting points and the progress they are making over time.	Is a starting points assessment carried out when the children start? Do you discuss this with the parents to identify any discrepancies between what a child may be doing at home and in the setting?
	If as part of the starting points assessment a child is seen to be making less progress in one of the prime areas, what action do you/would you take?
	What strategies do you use to track children's progress over time? How do you act on this information?
	What action would you take if a child suddenly started to make less progress?
Support those children who are disadvantaged or underperforming to catch up.	How do you use EYPP funding?
	Do you use individual learning plans? How have they been effective to support children?
	What is the key carer role in supporting these children to catch up?
	How do you involve parents in supporting their children in this instance?
	Do you liaise with outside agencies?
Help children to work at typical levels of development for their age, including those whose development exceeds what is typical for their age.	Do practitioners have a good base knowledge of child development? Are they aware of the appropriate development for the age phases of the children they work with in relation to the areas of learning and development?
	Do you have a gifted and talented scheme and are you able to encourage children who achieve beyond expectations to progress further?
	How do you challenge children to extend learning?
	How do you meet the needs of pre-school children prior to them starting school?
Help children to develop skills that will help them to be ready for the next stage of learning.	Do you discuss with the children their progress and look at how they have moved on, perhaps using photographs.
	How are children enabled to move forward and reach their potential. Do you enable children to explore freely in a stimulating environment so it is clear to see their natural abilities?
	How do you prepare for the transition between rooms in a day nursery?
	How do you prepare children for school? Do you have school uniform for role play, use display, photos of the schools and teachers, a school role play?

The inspection day

Where a previous judgement was **Inadequate**, check for monitoring letters, note whether any actions or recommendations were raised as a result of monitoring visits and identify whether any outstanding actions or recommendations need to be checked. Update information about the setting – inspectors must not simply cut and paste information from old reports as things may have changed.

Check whether the providers have a web page. This may contain useful information and give access to self-evaluation and improvement plans. Make sure your compliance records are ready and accessible (see checklist below).

So the inspector has arrived, what should you do? The most important thing is to carry on as normal (once you've got over the first feelings of 'they're here'!). Carrying on and treating it as a normal day ensures stability for the children and that you will be showing yourselves at your best to the

Compliance checklist for inspection

- ☐ Record of Disclosure and Barring Service (DBS) checks.
- ☐ Environmental health checks.
- ☐ Risk assessments.
- ☐ Policies and procedures file.
- ☐ SEF.
- ☐ Development plan.
- ☐ Records of conversation with local authority.
- ☐ Selection of recruitment records and references.
- ☐ Qualifications and training record including first aid and safeguarding.
- ☐ Training matrix and records.
- ☐ Sample of induction and professional development record.
- ☐ Complaints record.
- ☐ Staff meeting minutes and agenda.
- ☐ Accident and incidents record.
- ☐ Sample of planning and assessment records (in room linked to tracked children).
- ☐ Register (in room).
- ☐ Medicine record.
- ☐ Fire drill record and evaluation.
- ☐ EYPP evidence.

What the inspector will do on arrival

- ■ Check you have been informed.
- ■ Introduce themselves and show their identification passbook.
- ■ Ask you to display a notice that inspection is taking place.
- ■ Make arrangements to talk to parents.
- ■ Make arrangements for a longer meeting with you.
- ■ Refer to any concerns that have led to this inspection – confidentiality should be maintained to protect sensitive information.
- ■ Confirm the accuracy of information – inspectors must check all staff qualifications and record them in their toolkit.
- ■ Agree a timetable for inspection activities including joint observations.
- ■ Ask for your self-evaluation where you haven't submitted it and confirm dates submitted information was completed.
- ■ Ask you about different groups of children attending the setting e.g boys, girls, children with significantly low starting points, children with English as second language, funded two-year-olds etc.
- ■ Make arrangements for feedback at the end of the inspection.
- ■ Tour the premises following up with any issues arising from tour.
- ■ In group provision only the inspector will ask the manager to contact the provider so that they can be present during feedback.
- ■ In some cases the inspector may make arrangements for extra meetings with SENCO or person responsible for child protection.
- ■ Confirm arrangements for joint observations in group provision.

Have ready an Ofsted file/box of things you are proud of and want to share with the inspector from the past 12 months.

inspector. What you don't want is the inspector to hear a member of staff saying to you or someone else "why are you doing that?", implying that what is happening is not normal practice.

Be as accommodating as possible, remember the inspector will have a laptop with them to record their observations and findings, and therefore will need space in each room. It is probably worth mentioning at this point that the inspector is not there to look for negatives, but will be looking to see how you demonstrate that the Early Years Foundation Stage (EYFS) is in practice in your setting.

Your staff team will need support and may well be feeling particularly nervous. It is important they feel reassured, particularly after being asked questions by the inspector.

How to support your staff team during an inspection:

You'll know your team, so you'll know who will be unfazed by the inspector arriving and who might be nervous.

To alleviate the panicking, you just need to carry on as normal and give reassurance as necessary.

Introduce members of staff confidently to the inspector and mention their role in the setting and the level of qualification, as well as their name.

Also make sure that the kettle is always ready to boil, there are plenty of clean mugs and milk ready for staff during their breaks!

What about if you have doubts about your inspector?

Your doubts might be about general awareness, competency, conduct and level of professionalism.

It is very unlikely that this would happen, but there are few steps to follow if this should occur. Talk to another senior member of staff to see if they have doubts as well.

If you feel you do have cause for concern and that the inspection judgment might be compromised, you should talk to the inspector, so the situation can hopefully be resolved there and then. If you are not happy with the outcome of this conversation, you should phone Ofsted on 08456 404040. Formal complaints can be made at any stage during the inspection or up to thirty calendar days from the date of publication of any report.

Feedback

So, the inspection is over and you're about to receive your feedback from the inspection. Take a couple of deep breaths and remember the following:

- Make sure you go somewhere quiet for the feedback, and ensure staff know not to interrupt you.

- Listen carefully.

- Jot down key points.

- Ask questions to help your understanding and to clarify points.

- If you're unclear about something ask for specific examples to help understanding.

- Acknowledge the feedback.

- Try not to focus just on any negatives but remember the positives as well and see the negatives as points for developing and improving practice.

- Take time to sort out in your head what has been said before feeding back to the rest of the staff team.

Remember feedback is two-way and if you feel you have justification to challenge something that has been said, then do so clearly, concisely and with evidence which can be verbally explained. Then you still will feel confident about it after the inspector has gone.

Unless the outcome of the inspection was inadequate or you have been given a time limit on certain points for action, give yourself a few days grace to digest all that has been said. Having given yourself this time, you will then be in a better position to take action on the points raised and identifying how to move forward and improve with your practice.

Meeting between the inspector and the provider

As part of the inspection, the inspector will want to meet with the provider or manager. It will be at a convenient time for the setting, usually near the start of the inspection, so anything discussed can be followed up.

In a childminding setting or a group setting operating from one room e.g. a pre-school in a village hall, the meeting will most likely take place when the children are engaged and when appropriate during the general observations of the setting. Obviously, the inspector will recognise that you will still have to supervise the children and meet their needs. In a setting where the provider/manager is supernumerary and the meeting takes place in another room or office, the meeting should take no longer than an hour and will probably be much shorter.

If the manager or nominated person has changed since the last inspection, the inspector will need to ensure that the provider meets the requirements of the EYFS. The inspector will need to establish that roles and responsibilities are clear for the manager and/or provider, this will include the provider's legal accountability.

The initial discussion will refer to issues being followed up during the inspection and times should be agreed for further discussion, so that the inspector can feedback to the provider.

The inspector will evaluate the following:

- Whether the leaders' and managers' roles are clearly established and whether they meet and understand the requirements of the EYFS.

- How well the planning, assessment and delivery of the areas of learning and development are monitored and the extent to which children's needs are identified and met through appropriate intervention.

- The effectiveness of staff supervision, appraisal, performance management, training and ongoing professional development.

- The effectiveness of the providers plans for driving improvement in the quality of teaching and children's achievements, particularly the most vulnerable.

- How self evaluation is used in identifying and informing priorities and setting challenging targets for improvement. This will include how the views of parents, children and any partners contribute to self evaluation and progress towards any actions raised at the last inspection or monitoring visit.

- The consistency of practice and how standards are set and maintained.

- How effective the setting is in working with other professionals and partnership work needed to support children with identified needs.

- Safeguarding policies, procedures and effectiveness, including child protection procedures, risk assessments, staff recruitment procedures and staff supervision.

The variety of observations the inspector may use during the inspection

- Observation of a specific activity or age group for around 20 to 30 minutes. This will enable the inspector to see several practitioners and help them to gauge whether the seven areas of learning and development are all reflected in what is on offer to the children. They will also be able to see how children of different ages/stages of development/abilities are supported. For pre-school aged-three and -four children, the inspector will observe how their literacy skills are developing and how ready the older children are for school.

- Tracking a small group of children to assess their experiences (see opposite).

- Longer observations, over 30 minutes, this is particularly relevant in baby rooms, where it may be necessary in order to observe care

The views of the parent/carer

- Where possible during inspection the inspector must find out the views of the parents. This should include any parent who asks to speak to them. This will contribute to the judgement and on how well the setting works in partnership with parents.

- The inspector will set aside time when most parents arrive or depart to talk to them. The inspector must not miss opportunities to talk to parents.

- If the timing of inspection means that inspectors cannot talk to parents in person they must check how the provider obtains and uses the views of parents – if this cannot be demonstrated then the inspector will need to consider if the provision is inadequate or requires improvement.

routines, attachments and activities. This type of observation may also be used to capture best practice or to get a clearer insight into weaker practice to provide evidence to support recommendations.

- Short observations of several activities, this is often used when the children are in one room and move around the activities depending on their interests.

Joint observations: the inspector and provider observing together

In group settings the inspector will invite the provider or a nominated senior member of staff to join them in one or more observations of activities, care routines and/or scrutiny of children's progress. It is entirely up to the provider whether or not they wish to participate. There are pros and cons.

Ofsted feel that joint observations help them to:

■ Get clear understanding of the provider's accuracy and skills in monitoring and evaluation of practice and professional development programme for practitioners.

Ofsted also feel it gives the provider an opportunity to contribute to the evidence used to make judgements about the provision.

The inspector should be mindful of overloading the provider or senior management. If the provider declines the opportunity to do a joint observation this should be recorded in the evidence base along with the reason given.

Points to consider and remember

■ You and the inspector need to agree what is to be observed.

■ After the observation, they should discuss their views of what has been seen in relation to the quality of the practice. The inspector will expect the provider/manager to give their views first considering the strengths, what went well and what could have made it better and a general summation.

■ If the practice observed is weak, the inspector will ask you the provider/manager what action you are taking if any or what action you will take to improve the practice. The inspector will discuss with you when and how to feedback to the practitioner, the inspector may wish to observe your feedback.

■ If you write your observation, the inspector must look at this, and any differences should be discussed. Notes you make will not be taken away or used as a basis for evidence, although the inspector may refer to them in their evidence.

■ Where childminders work alone e.g. without an assistant, the inspector may observe a specific activity planned by the childminder and discuss the aims and learning objectives of the activity, this would then be followed up after the activity discussing what the child has gained from the experience and what their next steps would be.

The inspector tracking children as part of the inspection

During an inspection an inspector will track at least two children during their time in the setting. This will help them decide how well the setting meets individual needs, facilitates next steps and monitors progress. As part of this process the inspector will want to look at the tracked children's records e.g. learning journey and talk to the relevant key carers.

Preparation

This can be quite a daunting prospect for practitioners, so it is essential that the leader in the setting prepares staff

During the inspection

■ The inspector should hold brief discussions to let you know of emerging inspection findings – these meetings will be recorded as part of the evidence.

■ Before the end of the inspection the inspector will check again if there is any further evidence they would like to submit.

■ The inspector should diagnose where improvements should be made and how these may be implemented.

■ Where it appears that a setting may be judged as inadequate there should be an early discussion with the provider – although the inspector does not make final judgements until the end of the inspection.

for this, to boost confidence. This is achieved by:

- Including tracking of children and questioning as part of the staff observation and supervision cycle.

- Ensuring staff are confident in the planning cycle involved.

- Ensuring all staff are confident and up-to-date in their knowledge of the EYFS.

- That there are robust systems in place for monitoring the educational programme.

How the inspector will select the children

The inspector must track a minimum of two children, this will increase where there are a wide range of children, where children are in different rooms, where there are distinct groups of children and in larger settings.

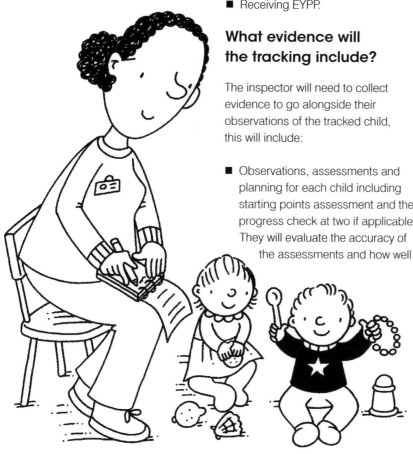

They will identify children who have attended the setting for a reasonable amount of time, so that starting points have been established and progress has been evaluated. In the sample of tracked children, the inspector may include:

- A baby.

- A funded two-year-old.

- A boy and girl who are soon to transfer to school.

- Children the provision identifies as having differing abilities.

- A looked-after child, if applicable.

- A child with disabilities and/or special educational needs.

- A child who speaks English as an additional language.

- A boy and/or a girl from any groups, who may be disadvantaged.

- Receiving EYPP.

What evidence will the tracking include?

The inspector will need to collect evidence to go alongside their observations of the tracked child, this will include:

- Observations, assessments and planning for each child including starting points assessment and the progress check at two if applicable. They will evaluate the accuracy of the assessments and how well

the children's next steps in learning are planned.

- Discussion with the child's key person about the child and their progress.

- They will look at records the setting has that show how the child's progress has been tracked and include any concerns about development in the prime and/or specific areas of learning.

What will they observe the tracked child doing?

To help support the evaluations made, based on the evidence as detailed above, they will observe the following in relation to the child:

- The range of activities the child takes part in, considering if they are solitary, with others, self-initiated or adult-led.

- The quality and appropriateness of adults' interventions and interactions.

- The level of challenge available for the child in relation to their age/stage of development.

- The development levels at which the children are working including whether they are exceeding, reaching, or likely to reach typical levels of development for their age.

- Ways in which communication and language are developed and literacy taught.

- Whether children are developing skills in the prime areas that help them to be ready for school.

- How well any learning they demonstrate is built upon by the adults working with them.

- The children's care arrangements, including intimate care, the levels of privacy afforded the child, supervision arrangements for the child and for the adult undertaking personal hygiene tasks.

Assessment by the inspector of children's progress

The inspector needs to determine if the children are making progress and how well this is tracked and monitored. Children's progress relates mainly to the ability of the practitioners to identify individual needs and appropriate next steps and how this is demonstrated in knowledge and understanding of each child's learning and development.

The assessment of children's progress will begin from their starting points, taking into account how long they have been at the setting and how often they attend, their individual needs, looking at how the provision gathers information about what the children know and their progress towards the early learning goals.

The inspector will use the evidence they have gathered to evaluate how well the provider and practitioners know the children, understand them and the progress they are making. They will also want to see whether the adults have appropriately high expectations for the children, and if the learning gaps for children who are disadvantaged are narrowing. They will also want to ensure that children are at their expected levels of development.

The inspector will also consider the following as part of the assessment:

- The practitioner's knowledge and understanding of the EYFS.

- How and when parents/carers are asked for information about their child's development. How often summaries of the practitioner's observations are shared with parents and carers.

- Can practitioners reliably identify those children whose learning and development is not at the expected developmental band, either because they are working above or below the expected level and what is being done to support these children.

- How the SENCO is involved where there are concerns about a child.

- Any changes made to activities/resources/routines/the environment as a result of observations, and evaluations of the impact of those changes.

Inspection and the EYPP (Early Years Pupil Premium)

The inspectors will want evidence of how the EYPP has been spent and why you chose to spend it in this way. They will expect you to have researched your decision to optimise impact on the child.

At least one child receiving EYPP will be amongst these chosen to be tracked.

At the end of the inspection

- The inspector should invite the provider to meet to:

  - Discuss any inadequate or outstanding practice seen.

  - Ensure that you understand how the evidence meets the judgements which will be linked to the Evaluation Schedule statements.

  - Allow you to raise any concerns.

  - Alert you in the event of any serious concerns.

- The inspector should ensure that you understand actions and recommendations and that you have the opportunity to comment on the draft wording.

- Actions and recommendations should be precise, specific and detailed.

- The inspector must set aside time after the inspection to consider evidence and make final judgements.

- If the inspector has any concerns about their judgement they should contact their service helpdesk.

- The inspector should also allow time to prepare feedback – making certain that their evidence is clear and irrefutable and supports judgements.

- Before leaving the setting the inspector must give formal feedback in professional and objective language.

- The inspector must ensure before leaving that you are clear about judgements.

- Judgements are confidential until confirmed.

- If you receive an inadequate you have to inform your local authority straight away.

Practitioners and the inspection

Gathering and recording evidence

53. Inspectors must spend as much time as possible gathering evidence about the quality of teaching and learning by:

- observing the children at play

- talking to the children and practitioners about the activities provided

- observing the interactions between practitioners and children

- gauging children's levels of understanding and their engagement in learning

- talking to practitioners about their assessment of children's knowledge, skills and abilities and how they are extending them

- observing care routines and how they are used to support children's personal development

- evaluating the practitioners' knowledge of the early years curriculum.

54. In **group provision**, the inspector **must** track the experience and development levels of a representative sample of children. The inspector must track at least two children. The inspector should discuss with the provider the relevant children's starting points, looking at any assessment evidence the setting provides and the children's progress. The evidence collected **must** refer to:

- the quality of the practitioners' assessment knowledge of each child

- the progress check for any children aged two

- the impact of any early years pupil premium funding on the children's progress

- the discussions held with each child's key person and information about progress

- any records the provision keeps that show how they have tracked the progress children make, including recording any concerns about the

children's development in the prime or specific areas of learning or both

- whether children are developing skills in the prime areas that help them to be ready for their next stage of education, including school.

Observation and discussion

63. Inspectors must not advocate a particular method of planning, teaching or assessment. They must not look for a preferred methodology but must record aspects of teaching and learning they consider are effective and identify ways in which it can be improved.

Watford LRC

64. Inspectors will not expect practitioners to prepare documentation for the inspection. They will use the evidence gathered from observations to help judge the overall quality of the curriculum provided for children.

65. Inspectors must spend most of the inspection time gathering first-hand evidence by observing the quality of the daily routines and activities of children and staff. These observations enable inspectors to judge the contribution practitioners make to children's learning, progress, safety and well-being. They should enable them to collect sufficient evidence to support detailed and specific recommendations about improvement needed to teaching and learning, personal development, behaviour and welfare, and leadership and management.

66. In group settings, inspectors should observe as many staff members as possible to ensure that an accurate picture of the overall quality of interactions between practitioners and children can be gained.

67. When observing interactions between staff and children, inspectors should consider how well staff:

- engage in dialogue with children

- watch, listen and respond to children

- model language

- encourage children to express their thoughts and use new words

- support independence and confidence

- encourage children to speculate and test ideas through trial and error

- enable children to explore and solve problems

- behave as an excellent role model for children to copy

- support children to recognise and respond to their own physical needs

- attend to children's personal needs

- deal with children's care arrangements, including intimate care, the levels of privacy afforded to children, and supervision arrangements when undertaking personal hygiene tasks.

68. Inspectors will also discuss children's development with staff as part of the inspection, Much of this will be through incidental conversations, promoted by observing the children at play and the interactions between them and adults.

From Early Years Inspection Handbook (August 2015) ref: 150068.

After the inspection

help gain an insight into the experience and impact of change.

'Effects of change' questionnaire

Think of any changes you have experienced.

- How did you feel?

- How would you have preferred to experience the change (if negative) OR what made the change successful (if positive)?

- Why do you think someone introduced the change in the first place?

- Was it what you wanted or needed?

- Should your opinions count? Why?

When a change is planned or introduced the first thing that people ask themselves is how will this change affect me? This is particularly relevant if the change is presented to them with no discussion or explanation.

Change that is to be implemented after an inspection concerns everyone and therefore should involve everyone. This is essential if the change is going to be implemented successfully and have a positive impact on the setting. Even if the only involvement is being part of a discussion about how to move forward and work to implement action points.

For people to be accepting of change, you need to be able to answer how the change will affect them, as well as involve them to some degree in

---

Remember: it may take up to three weeks to receive confirmation of your official Ofsted outcome.

Your inspection is over, so what should you do apart from breathe a huge sigh of relief? First, and most importantly, celebrate the successes of the inspection and identified areas of strength. This should involve every member of staff, as they will have all contributed to this. Make sure you tell the parents and carers of the children in your setting and why not generate some positive publicity by contacting your local paper?

Once the euphoria and sense of relief is over, you will need to sit down quietly without any distractions and read the report and identify what is being said. Regardless of the grading outcome of the inspection, there will be changes that you should implement as part of the setting's

continual development. This includes settings with an outstanding grading.

This might be particularly difficult if your inspection didn't go well or you were unhappy with the outcome. Your first impulse reaction might be to blame Ofsted, to blame yourself or another member of staff. It may take a while to be able to look at action points and outcomes with the perspective required. It is essential you reach the point of objectivity to be able to move forward. Don't blame anyone, including yourself, instead work on moving forward.

Part of moving forward is bound to involve change. By nature we are resistant to change so managers and leaders in settings need to look carefully at how they implement this change.

To begin with, it might be useful to answer questions in the box below to

the planning of the change. This involvement helps to ensure that the change is implemented successfully and that the action points become part of practice.

Reasons for a resistance to change

- A desire not to lose something of value.

- A misunderstanding of the change and its implications.

- A belief that it doesn't make sense.

- A low tolerance for change – fear of not being able to develop new skills and behaviour required of them.

Managing successful change

- Keep the lines of communication open.

- If you can consult with the team, do.

- Be prepared to listen to concerns and respond appropriately.

- Give explanations and reasons.

- Ensure the team know the benefits and implications of the change and specifically how it affects their job role.

- Be honest about the expected effect of change.

- Review the effect of change after implementation.

To implement the change effectively and monitor the process of implementation and the outcome, you need to set Specific, Measurable, Achievable, Realistic and Time-bound (SMART) targets and devise an action plan, as discussed in the chapter on reflective practice.

Moving forward after an inspection is essential, the temptation will be to sit back and think 'oh we don't need to worry about that for another three years.' For any development of practice and skills to become embedded in the day-to-day you need to start as soon as possible. This will then help to ensure you reap the benefits at your next inspection. Most importantly, it means that you are providing the best possible early years experience for the children who attend your setting.

Remember to inform Ofsted if…

- There is a change of leader/person in charge in your setting, even if this is only temporary e.g. maternity leave.

- If there is a change of any address at which you provide childcare.

- If there is any significant event that is likely to affect the suitability of any person, who has reached the age of 16 and lives or works on the premises, to be in contact with children.

- The injury, serious accident or death of a child occurs whilst they are receiving registered childcare.

- The injury, serious accident or death to any other person on the premises on which the registered childcare is provided.

- If a child receiving childcare has a sudden serious illness.

- If there is any allegation of serious harm to or abuse of a child committed:

  ☐ By a person caring for children on the premises, whether the allegation relates to harm or abuse that occurred on those premises or elsewhere.

  ☐ By any person, where the allegation relates to harm or abuse that occurred on the premises.

- If there is any incident of food poisoning affecting two or more children cared for on the premises.

- If you wish to change the terms of

your registration e.g. increase the number of children you care for.

Additionally, if you are a childminder, inform Ofsted if...

- A person in your household turns 16.

- You employ an assistant.

- An adult moves in or out of your house.

- You wish to build an extension to your house.

- It is essential to inform Ofsted of any of the above, as failure to do so is likely to impact on the outcome of an inspection.

Inspection reports

The format for inspection reports has changed – they are now much clearer to read and give indicators of what you are doing well and where you can improve and develop your practice.

- The top of the report will clearly identify what grade you got for each of the four outcomes and your overall grade.

- There will then be a series of bullet points stating what is working well in your setting.

- Followed by the reason why you are not yet at a higher grade. If you are Outstanding, this section is omitted.

- There will be a list of what the inspector did during the visit e.g. what they observed, if they spoke to any parents, what paperwork they looked at and anything else they checked.

- There is an explanation of what you may need to do to meet the requirements of the EYFS and how you can further improve the quality of your provision.

- Finally, a description of the inspector's judgements on the four outcomes.

With thoughtful preparation and using this book, your EYFS inspection can be a positive and stress-free experience. Remember, with or without an inspection we can always develop and improve our practice, and aim to provide the best possible service.

Further resources

Publications

Early Years Inspection Handbook (Ofsted, 2015, ref: 150068)

Teaching and Play in the Early Years – a balancing act? (Ofsted, 2015, ref: 150085)

Inspecting Safeguarding in the early years, education and skills settings (Ofsted, 2015, ref: 150067)

Confident, Capable and Creative: Supporting Boys' Achievements (DCSF, 2007).

Inclusion Development Programme: Supporting Children with Speech, Language and Communication Needs – Guidance for Practitioners in the Early Years Foundation Stage (DCSF, 2008).

Key Elements of Effective Practice (KEEP) (DFES, 2005).

Safeguarding and Child Protection in the Early Years (Practical Pre-School Books, 2012).

Social and Emotional Aspects of Development: Guidance for Practitioners Working in the Early Years Foundation Stage (DCSF, 2008).

Supporting Children Learning English as an Additional Language (DCSF, 2007).

The Criminal Records Bureau Code of Practice and Explanatory Guide. The Data Protection Act 2003.

The Disability Discrimination Act 2005.

The Early Years Foundation Stage in Practice (Practical Pre-School Books, revised 2012).

The Vetting and Barring Scheme (Independent Safeguarding Authority, 2009).

Childcare Groups: A Passion to be Outstanding (Ofsted, 2009).

Childminders: A Passion to be Outstanding (Ofsted, 2009).

Good Practice Guides – continually updated (www.ofsted.gov.uk).

Progress Matters: Reviewing and Enhancing Young Children's Development (DSCF, 2009).

Every Child A Talker: Guidance for Early Language Lead Practitioners (DSCF, 2009).

Building Futures: Believing in Children – A Focus on Provision for Black Children in the Early Years (DSCF, 2009).

Early Years Observation and Planning in Practice (Practical Pre-School Books, revised edition 2012).

Websites

www.foundationyears.org.uk

www.education.gov.uk

www.education.gov.uk/ofsted